# A Top f

Liz sat on the rug.

Liz had a big, red rag.

"I will cut it up."

"I will cut a red top for Zig!" Liz cut the red rag up. Liz got a pin to fit the top on to Zig.

Did the top fit? The top was big. It was a bad job. Zig got a jab in his rib. Zig was sad.

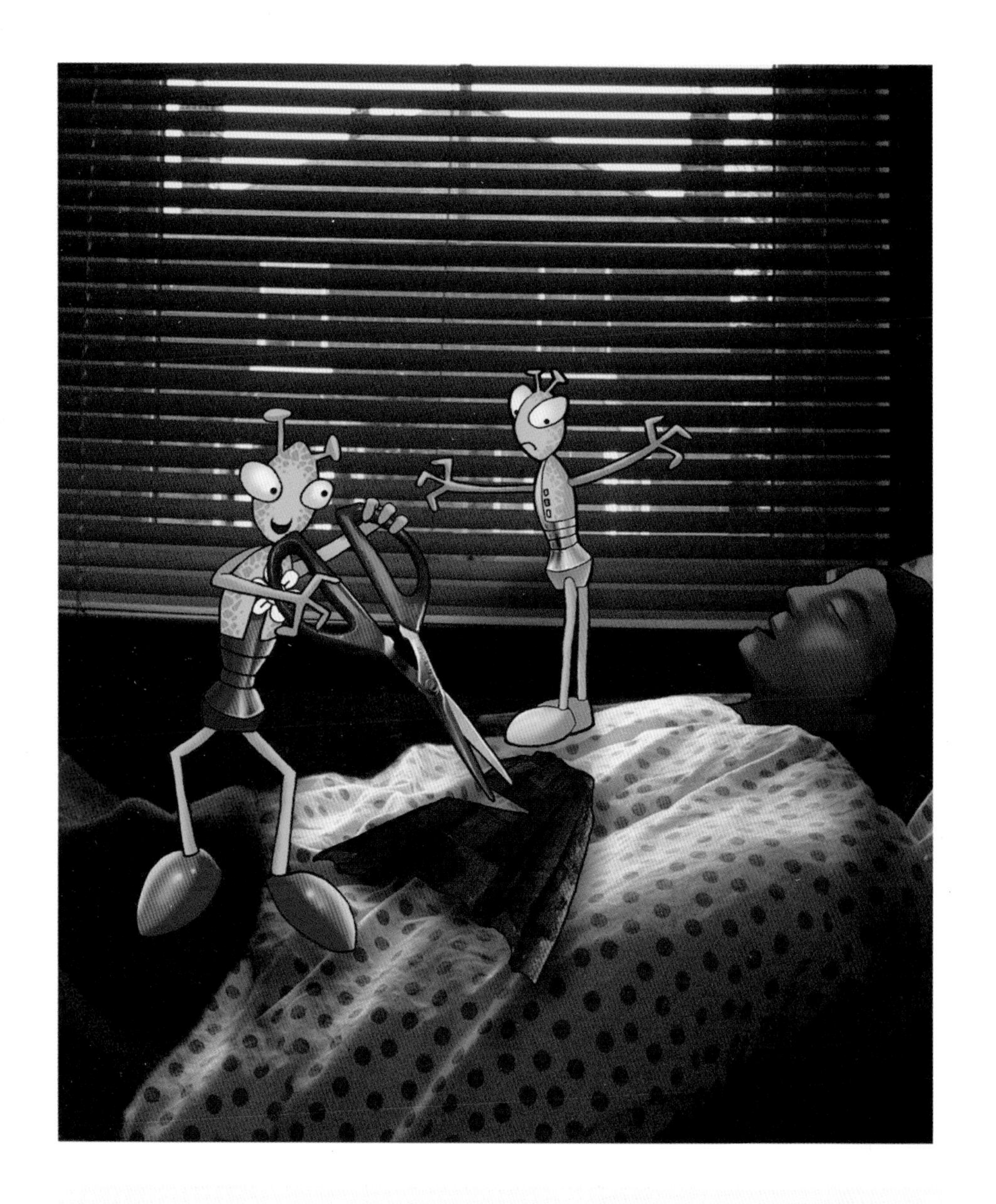

Liz got in to bed. Zig was fed up. Zog got the pin off.
"I will fit the top on to Zig."

Zap! Zig had a red top on.
Zap! The red top had a big,
red zip. It was not a bad job.

Zig got the red rag and cut a red top for Zog. The top had a zip. Zig and Zog had fun on the jet.

# Game page

On the next page is a game for two to help you practise reading the words in this book.

Photocopy the page twice and cut up one page to make word cards.

Cut the other page in half to make two base cards. Place the word cards face down on the table.

Take turns to pick up a card.

Say the word.

Place the matching word card on your base card. If you do not have the word on your base card, put it back face down with the other cards.

The winner is the first one to fill their base card!